thanks mum

thanks mum

inspiring thoughts for mothers

www.youaretheauthor.com

Published in the UK in 2003 exclusively for
WHSmith Limited
Greenbridge Road
Swindon SN3 3LD
www.WHSmith.co.uk
by Tangent Publications, an imprint of
Axis Publishing Limited.

Conceived and created by
Axis Publishing Limited
8c Accommodation Road
London NW11 8ED
www.axispublishing.co.uk

Creative Director: Siân Keogh
Managing Editor: Brian Burns
Production Manager: Tim Clarke

ISBN 0–9543620–6–3

2 4 6 8 10 9 7 5 3

Printed and bound in China

about this book

Thanks Mum brings together an inspirational selection of powerful and life-affirming phrases about mothers and motherhood and combines them with evocative and gently amusing animal photographs that bring out the full humour and pathos of the human condition.

We all lead busy lives and sometimes forget to tell our mums how much we love them and how grateful we are for everything they do for us. These inspiring examples of wit and wisdom, written by real people based on their true-life experiences, sum up the essence of motherhood, and why our mothers will always be so special to us. As one of the entries so aptly puts it – mothers make the world go around.

So give thanks to your mum and tell her you love her!

about the author

Why have one author when you can have the world? This book has been compiled using the incredible resource that is the world wide web. From the many hundreds of contributions that were sent to the website, *www.youaretheauthor.com*, we have selected the ones that best sum up what being a mum is all about – giving support, encouragement and, most of all, love.

Please continue to send in your special views, feelings and advice about life – you never know, you too might see your wise words in print one day!

www.youaretheauthor.com

A mother's love
is like a circle.
It has no beginning
and no ending.

anon@youaretheauthor.com

A mother's love is forever;
time, distance, hardship...
all fall before the
strength of her love.

I'm frequently amazed that my
mother will call, knowing that I'm
worried, even though I live
hundreds of miles away.

anon@youaretheauthor.com

You never realize how much your mother loves you till you explore the attic – and find every letter you ever sent her, every finger painting, clay pot, bead necklace, Easter chicken, cardboard Santa Claus, paperlace Mother's Day card and school report since day one.

There is no friendship, no love like that of the mother for her child.

My mother may often question
what I do or say, but her love is,
I know, unquestionable.

Thomas_Elliot@hotmail.com

No language could express the power and beauty and heroism of a mother's love.

anon@youaretheauthor.com

A mother is a blend of
strength and survivorship,
experience and insight,
fancy and reflection.

anon@youaretheauthor.com

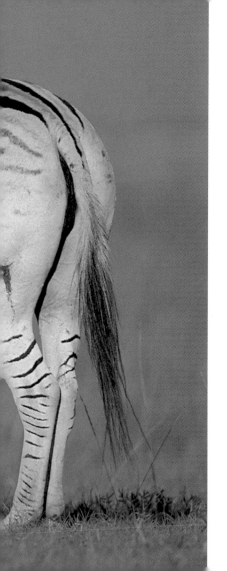

A mother is not a person to lean on, but a person to make leaning unnecessary.

I've always known that no matter what happens, no matter what I do, my mother will be there.

stephanie_frances@yahoo.co.uk

You're never too heavy for your mother to bear.

But try, as you get older, to swap roles once in a while.

Abi37@hotmail.com

The best mothers are
those who listen, and
always understand.

A mother
understands what
a child does
not say.

anon@youaretheauthor.com

A mother laughs our
laughter, sheds our tears,
returns our love and
fears our fears.

Mother is the one to whom you hurry when you are troubled.

My mum is the best –
she's a friend when I need one,
a nurse when I need one,
and she's always there.

saffyshar@hotmail.com

A mother is like an island in life's ocean, a peaceful quiet shelter from the restless tide.

anon@youaretheauthor.com

Nobody knows how to
pamper like a mum.

Remember, though, you should
learn the lesson not just reap
the benefits.

saramatthews12@hotmail.com

Mother's arms are made up of tenderness, and sweet sleep blesses the child who lies therein.

This is your first refuge in life,
but its warmth and comfort
endure – all you need do is tap
into the memory.

melanie_williams_2@hotmail.com

A mother's love perceives no impossibilities.

brandon_top@musician.org

Mother love is the
fuel that enables
a normal human
being to do the
impossible.

anon@youaretheauthor.com

Like kites without strings, mothers teach you to soar with your dreams.

melanie_williams_2@hotmail.com

A mother's love is so strong and unyielding that it endures all circumstances: good fortune and misfortune, prosperity and privation, honour and disgrace.

anon@youaretheauthor.com

A mother is a person who seeing there are only four pieces of pie for five people, promptly announces she never did care for pie.

The way to your mother's heart,
is to eat her food with relish.
(Or anything else that
disguises the taste.)

The heart of a
mother is a deep
abyss at the
bottom of which
you will always find
forgiveness.

A mother loves her children even when they least deserve to be loved.

And Heaven knows, there have been times when I surely didn't deserve it!

anon@youaretheauthor.com

A mother's love is not
blind; it's just very
nearsighted.

It's not easy being a mother.
If it were easy, fathers
would do it.

A man's work is from
sun to sun, but a mother's
work is never done.

A mother always has
to think twice:
once for herself
and once for her child.

anon@youaretheauthor.com

Life is nothing but
a series of crosses
for mothers.

But that doesn't mean she isn't
prepared to bear them.

anon@youaretheauthor.com

The joys of
motherhood are
never fully
experienced
until the children
are in bed.

Geoffrey_Howarth@hotmail.com

If evolution really works,
how come mothers only have
one pair of hands?

Don't worry – they learned to
compensate by multi-tasking.

mike_pritch20@yahoo.com

Any mother could
perform the jobs of
several air traffic
controllers with ease.

By and large, mothers and housewives are the only workers who do not have regular time off.

And there's no such thing as flexi-time, part-time or job-share either.

anon@youaretheauthor.com

Being a full-time mother is one
of the highest-salaried jobs,
since the payment is pure love.

A mother who is
really a mother is
never free.

A mother holds her
children's hands for a while,
their hearts forever.

So do your best not to
weigh too much.

anon@youaretheauthor.com

A man loves his sweetheart the most, his wife the best, but his mother the longest.

Youth fades, love droops, the
leaves of friendship fall;
a mother's secret hope
outlives them all.

When I doubt myself, I think about
how much my mother believes in
me and it's astonishing how much
more confident I feel.

Geoffrey_Howarth@hotmail.com

Children and mothers never truly
part – they are bound in the
beating of each other's heart.

anon@youaretheauthor.com

The mother's heart is the child's schoolroom.

Thomas_Elliot@hotmail.com

Real mothers know that
a child's growth is not
measured by height
or years or grades.

It is marked by the
progression of Mama
to Mummy to Mother.

anon@youaretheauthor.com

Men are what their
mothers made them.

No matter how old a mother is, she watches her middle-aged children for signs of improvement.

Because she knows we can always improve…

mark.sit@lycos.com

Mothers are like
fine collectibles –
as the years go by,
they increase
in value.

So don't let them gather dust!

mariollah@yahoo.com

Mothers are the only
goddesses in whom the
whole world believes.

Blind worship is not called for –
regular attendance will do.

anon@youaretheauthor.com

Mother is the name
for God on the lips
and in the hearts
of little children.

Maybe this is because she is
the first reality, the first that
we believe in, the first that
we know to be true.

anon@youaretheauthor.com

A mother is the one through
whom God whispers love
to his little children.

And, yes, sometimes that voice can
raise above a whisper, but only
because you're not listening.

Motherhood is a wonderful thing – what a pity to waste it on children.

brandon_top@musician.com

Of all the rights of women,
the greatest is to be a mother.

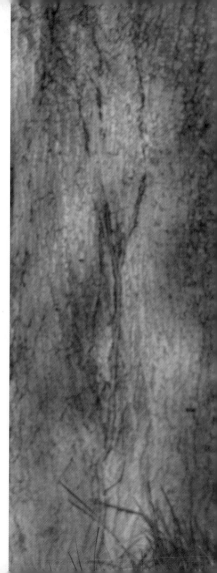

Simply having
children does not
make mothers.

That takes what happens
afterwards — for the rest
of your life.

anon@youaretheauthor.com

Mothers have as powerful an influence over the welfare of future generations as all other forces combined.

anon@youaretheauthor.com

Mothers make the family
go around.

Mothers make
the world go around.

Take the word 'family.' Strike out the 'm' for mother and the 'y' for youth – and all you have left is 'fail.'

anon@youaretheauthor.com

It takes a hundred
men to make an
encampment,
but one mum
to make a home.

Mother is the heartbeat
in the home.

A mother is she who can take the place of all others but whose place no one else can take.

A mother is a person who if she is not there when you get home from school you wouldn't know how to get your dinner, and you wouldn't feel like eating it anyway.

anon@youaretheauthor.com

Of all the things that come
in numbers – plenty of
rainbows, stars in the sky,
brothers, sisters, aunts,
uncles, cousins – you
have but one mother.

We only have one mum, one mummy, one mother in this world, one life. So give thanks and tell her you love her.

Without doubt, it is the gift that she will welcome most.

saffyshar@hotmail.com

I'll always love you, Mum.

sian.keogh@virgin.net